Season Of Preparation: Welcome to Season Of Preparation

Jacole Todd

Copyright © 2017 Jacole Todd
ISBN-13: 978-1542805599

All rights reserved. No part of this publication may be reproduced, stored in retrieval systems, or transmitted in any form or by any means—for example, electronic, photocopy, recording—without the prior written permission of the publisher. The only exception is brief quotations in printed reviews.

Unless otherwise indicated, Scripture is taken from the HOLY BIBLE, NEW INTERNATIONAL VERSION®, NIV®Copyright © 1973, 1978, 1984

ISBN: 1542805597

To my loving family—Michael, Vernia, Sheila, Hiram—and many other very supportive friends and family members. I praise God for my support system!

Contents

Acknowledgments

Preface

Introducing the Author 7

1. Welcome to Season of Preparation 11
2. Season of Preparation: The Genesis 16
3. Prayers for the Journey 28
4. A Time for Everything 37
5. Faith to Believe 42
6. Dealing with You 50
7. Be Healed 62
8. Lifting up the Father 71
9. Getting ready for Marriage 78
10. References 85

Acknowledgments

Acknowledgements go to my Heavenly Father who gave me this awesome assignment to bring Him glory. Words cannot express my gratitude for the many prayers, and the ladies and gentlemen who have supported *Season Of Preparation*.
God has placed some amazing people around me who express His love to me in so many ways.

Preface

Season Of Preparation is about my journey with the Lord. I am sharing some of the details of my life, in hopes that this will help you to be able to identify with me and see how my journey may encourage and enlighten you.

The book, Season of Preparation, Welcome to Season of Preparation, is an introduction into the journey of a woman, dealing with some of the circumstances that may come along with *life, relationships, emotions*, and the list goes on!

The reference keys listed below will help as you read through the book:

- Scripture References (SR)
  SR represents scriptures that are listed throughout the book. These scriptures are from the NIV version of the Bible. The references may be paraphrased, and on some occasions, the actual details of the scriptures are listed. There is a comprehensive list of scriptures in the reference section of the book.

- Lessons Learned
  Lessons Learned are lessons that I have learned throughout my *Season of Preparation*, that are highlighted throughout the book. There is a comprehensive list of lessons learned in the reference section of the book.

- T-Time
  T-Time stands for "My Testimony" and are sections throughout the book where I share some of my true feelings and perspectives from my experiences, and from my heart.

Introducing the Author: Jacole

Who Am I?

I have truly discovered me during this Season of Preparation…

My ongoing life and purpose

I am a woman who loves God, family, God's people, and who loves the institution of marriage. A common characteristic in our relationships is love and I believe that love should be shown in all that we do. I want love to always be exemplified in a major way.

My testimony and journey

My Season of Preparation journey has been somewhat of a rollercoaster that began at a beautiful climax of a really nice engagement ring from a man who I thought I would spend the rest of my life with…until the love of my life entered my heart.

Yes, you are reading this correct! I fell "head over heels" in love with another man, and my life has been changed forever. This man is Jesus Christ!

Now, my story may not be what you are thinking at this point and my story has not been a smooth, lovely bed of roses.

It has been a pretty bumpy road at times over the years; there have been both ups and downs/highs and lows. There has been rejection, fear, heartbreak/heartache, love, freedom, deliverance, and so on.

Many of these experiences have been captured within the pages of this book!

My current status

I am a 38 year-old single woman. It is very important for me to complete this book from the viewpoint of where I am today, September 16, 2016. I wanted to wait until I found my husband before completing this book, but I can't wait any longer.

I finally stepped out to finish this book, following the completion of a seven-day fast (for spiritual growth and development). During this time of reflection, study, and prayer, I realized that God is not going to allow me to move forward into the marriage that He has for me until I am obedient to Him. This means that my hands must be completely off the process of Him bringing my marriage to pass.

The list below contains a few of the actions that I must stop…

- "No crushes on men who I think are "the one."
- "No hoping and wishing every time a great man comes my way that he is my spouse."
- "No trying to figure out the meaning of everything when a new man comes into my life."

I must trust God, and lean not to my own understanding and tendencies to want to control everything. SR: Proverbs 3:5

His thoughts are not our thoughts, His ways are not our ways. SR: Isaiah 55:8

My history: Never forget where you came from…

I have desired to be married since age nineteen—I was in college, and my desire when I grew up was to "be a wife and a mother."

I wanted to produce people (children) who felt the same way about me that I felt about my parents (they are so awesome!). Little did I know that God had planned much more for me before my actual marriage would begin.

SR: Jeremiah 29:11—"I know the plans that I have for you," says the Lord.

What this book means to me

I began to write messages and excerpts for Season of Preparation in 2011 (five years ago), and actually started writing the book in 2013 (three years ago). There are several messages that will be listed under specific dates throughout the pages of this book—providing some details of my story that will be time specific, yet still very timely as you read through them.

I have often been embarrassed by my marital status, and I know that others have also felt this way—having to attend events and family gatherings without a significant other at your side. Marriage can often be viewed as a social status and others sometimes look at you in strange ways when you are single.

"Why aren't you married yet?" is a question that I have often been asked. This question used to make me feel sad at times. As I have continued to grow through this Season of Preparation (SOP), I have become more confident in God's process in my life—Him preparing me for the mate, and the marriage that He has for me.

The love of God covers and consumes me when I allow Him to—whether married or single—being in a relationship with God and experiencing His love is the only true status that I need.

This fact has kept me focused in the past; it is keeping me focused now, and will help me to remain focused in the future—even into my season of marriage.

As I lead you into this place called Season of Preparation, my desire is that you will have a safe place to grow, to develop, and to become who God has purposed you to be.

~SO, LET'S GO!~

1

Welcome to Season of Preparation

What is Season of Preparation?

So, that you can truly begin to understand what Season of Preparation is all about, I will break down each word of this phrase.

Let's start with the word *preparation*.

1) Preparation is defined as "getting ready." In life, no one likes to be caught off guard. Most people want to be ready or prepared for all that life brings their way. In reality, this may not be how things go. Life comes at us whether we are ready for it or not.

Preparation is an action word!

We are always in the process of preparing. As we prepare, we grow. As we grow, we move closer to where we have been destined to be from the beginning of time!

Now, let's look at the place of preparation.

    1. This can be a place of faith—getting to know who God is and who we are in Him.

2. This can be a place of joy—as you are expecting new things on the horizon.

3. This can be a place of development—learning and applying the lessons from what you have learned.

4. This can be a place of challenge—pushing you to move beyond your comfort zone and limitations that have been imposed on you by others or even from yourself.

Now, we all can be tempted to skip over preparation

Oftentimes, we would like to skip over preparation.

Laughing out loud (LOL)—I know that I do

<u>Why is this a temptation for many of us?</u>

One reason is that Preparation takes too long! Yes, preparation may seem to take a long time, but it is necessary.

Now, let's look at the word *season.*

---

2) A *season* is a distinct time frame, that is identified by specific characteristics.

Just like the four seasons within a year, seasons of life are designated by God and we do not have control over them. We cannot change them at our own will, and God has His timing for all seasons of life.

Dealing with the seasons of life

One key indicator of a season is time—the time that it may take to move through a season of life.

Many of us want to move through challenging seasons quickly to the place where we really desire to be.

It is usually not until we see that things are falling apart around us, that we realize that "we're in trouble". This is when we make the effort to get more knowledge and information about the specific season of life that we are in.

Well, this prolongs the process and can cause more harm than good!

Now, let's put it all together and look at the phrase *"Season of Preparation."*

---

3) *Season of Preparation* is a place. It is a safe place, a place of transparency, a place of healing, and a place of love.

It is a place to learn helpful principles and to prepare to use them along the journey toward a healthy relationship or a desired marriage. There are many helpful tools and resources that you can use during this time frame or season.

Where are you in your Season of Preparation?

As you are on the journey to your healthy relationship or marriage, Season of Preparation can help to guide you to healing, wholeness, understanding, comfort, and so much more. Season of Preparation does not just impact us on a personal level, but also, the impact can also extend to the society and our communities. Healthy versus unhealthy relationships can have lasting impacts on current as well as future generations in both positive and negative ways.

The Book: **Welcome to Season of Preparation**

This book encompasses brief excerpts and messages that are focused on the process of preparing for your healthy relationship or marriage, and finding hope, healing, faith, and purpose along the way. Although I am looking at things from a woman's perspective, I believe these are transferable principles of preparation that men can learn from as well.

The list of messages, prayers, and words of wisdom address some key areas that have come up in my life and in the lives of other single adults who desire to apply biblical principles and have healthy relationships as they live out their lives in purpose.

No, this is not a book on dating.

But this book can definitely be used to assist in the process of dating with the purpose of getting married.

No, I do not have all of the answers. (I wish I did!)

There are also many transferable principles that can help individuals from different walks of life. The relationship principles within this book can also provide insight and wisdom that can be applied to other areas of life.

Even if you are not a believer in Jesus Christ, or you are unsure of what this means and what it has to do with you, there still may be some words on the pages of this book that can be helpful for you.

I invite you to join me on this journey, My Journey! Maybe you will find yourself somewhere throughout this journey…Maybe you will be… <u>Encouraged</u>—<u>Empowered</u>…or even—<u>Enlightened</u>—as you take this Journey through Season of Preparation.

Come and embark upon this journey with me! Come along this Journey of Preparation!

~THIS IS THE SEASON OF PREPARATION!~

2

Season of Preparation: The Genesis

In the beginning…

An area where many single adults have challenges is, understanding marriage. What is marriage? Do I want to get married? How do I find a person to marry? How will I know if he or she is the right person for me? Why are so many people getting divorced?

This can be a very confusing and perplexing time in life.

This part of the book is a collection of some of the original messages that were written for *Season of Preparation*. These messages laid the foundation for *Season of Preparation* and are separated by the actual date the messages were recorded.

History: In the beginning—was my very first Season of Preparation message on November 23, 2011!

November 23, 2011

What I am learning this morning is that if I want to be able to encourage others in their marriages and family, I have to encourage my own marriage and family as well.

I must speak life into my marriage, even in the times when I cannot see any manifestation of it in my life and situations seem hopeless.

I have to pour into the vessel of my marriage and myself, allowing God to help and encourage me in this place. Yes, it is quite challenging, but no weapon formed against me and my marriage will prosper—no weapon, no mind-sets, no sins, no people! Not even myself or my future husband.

I will come into submission under God and into agreement with Him. In the matchless and powerful name of Jesus!

T-Time

This message was born in late November 2011. I was a bridesmaid in two weddings that year. Although I was extremely excited and happy for the two couples, whom I absolutely adore, I experienced quite a bit of internal turmoil a couple weeks before the second wedding.

During this time, I questioned myself and asked, *Why are you tripping?*

Through self-evaluation and talking things over with a friend, I realized that my issue was not with the wedding at all. My issue was with God and the time that it was taking for me to get married. I was disappointed and hurt about my process. After praying and accepting my true feelings, I was able to pull myself together (<u>Whew!</u>) The wedding was truly amazing!

Shortly after these events, I texted the November 23, 2011 message to a few of my single girlfriends. My desire was that they would be encouraged by the text.

Then over the next week, I texted more messages to my single girlfriends. I soon realized that I needed to stop sending the "random" text messages and began recording these messages in a journal…and Season of Preparation was born.

December 5, 2011

Obedience is key!

Ladies! Where the rubber meets the road is when you are faced with the ideal man, who appears to be from God.

You cannot forget all that God has taught you during this "Season of Preparation! (SOP)." Whether the man is truly your husband to be or not, obedience is key to you receiving the fullness of your blessing of marriage from God.

You have to make sure God is driving the relationship, not you or your man. I am praying for you, so please continue to pray for me! Let the Lord drive! Please! He is qualified to drive!

Lesson Learned
Let the Lord drive! Please! He is qualified to drive!

December 10, 2011

Be ready and honest!

1) Be ready when he comes…be in preparation mode.

2) Focus on your preparation process, and what this looks like for you!

3) Do things God's way and expect His results.

4) Let's be honest ladies (or gentlemen)! Do not pretend. Be honest with yourself about how you feel and who you are.

December 11, 2011

Addressing the "habit of settling"

Don't settle for less than God's best for you… God has great things in store for you, but you must trust Him.

A message to my single sisters (and brothers)…

My prayer is that the habit of settling will be removed from you in the name of Jesus…that no weapon formed against you shall prosper, but that you would walk in the fullness of all that you and God would have for you to be. Amen! SR: Isaiah 54:17

Lesson Learned
Don't settle for less than God's best for you…

We wrestle not against flesh and blood, but against powers, principalities, wickedness, and darkness in High Places.
SR: Ephesians 6:12

December 13, 2011

In the trenches: "The War Cry"

(It is time for battle!)

<u>In the trenches: Everyone cannot stand in the trenches with you…</u>

When you are fighting and going through challenges, you must make sure that you are accompanied by God and by the people who He allows (if anyone) to be there with you. You want people by your side who will pray with you, listen to you, share wisdom with you, and sometimes cry with you.

The truth is that we all need wisdom, support and guidance along our life journeys. God can provide this through others that He places in our lives or directly through His word and through prayer.

SR: Isaiah 54:17: No weapon formed against me shall prosper…

Lesson Learned
In the trenches: Everyone cannot stand in the trenches with you.

God's Word says…

    I am (your deliverer)
    I am (your peace)
    I am (your way maker)
    I am (your guidance)
    I am (your caring and loving Lord)
    I am (your source)
    I am (your wonderful counselor)
    I am (your partner in ministry)
    I am (your keeper)
    I am (your answer)
    I am (the lover of your soul)
    I am (your safety)
    I am (your rear guard)

In life's battles, it is always good to acknowledge that you actually are in battle, and be ready to fight.

T-Time

Lord, I want this so bad and believe that you have brought me here for such a time as this. There are many emotions that I have experienced along this journey. One emotion is fear of not finding the right person and the right relationship. Fear is never the appropriate response of faith. The two just simply do not go together; they are not a pair. I praise you Lord and thank you for my breakthrough in overcoming this area of fear!

December 14, 2011

My testimony: My genesis ...

Where it all begins...(The desire for marriage/covenant)

I am seeking Him *(My Lord)* on how He can use me to help restore families and marriages by contributing to the process of helping myself and others in the process of preparation before getting married.

This will aide in helping others make healthier, Christ-centered marriage decisions, and "be" healthier individuals prior to entering the marriage covenant. My focus is to help men, women and the youth to apply principles for building healthy relationships with themselves and others. This will be accomplished by providing resources, training, partnerships and other needed tools.

~~~~~~~~~~~~~~~~~~~~~~~~~~~~~~~~

December 15, 2011

Dealing with the desire for marriage

1) If you desire intimate companionship (physical, mental, emotional) of someone of the opposite sex, you probably desire biblical marriage.

2) If you allow space in your life for God's timing, the desire will not be fulfilled in the wrong way. The desire will be fulfilled when the time is right for both you and your spouse.

T-Time

My testimony

Sometimes, I can "jump the gun" and focus on what I want now, and not consider God at all. I can sometimes travel down the wrong road, but that is not my intention. I misunderstand things at times and my timing gets off from God's timing.

SR: Psalm 37:4: God gives you your heart's desires.

God knows the desires that are in your heart and He desires to give you the desires that are according to His will. He will bring your marriage to pass in the time that is best for both you and your spouse.

If the relationship is not in God's timing, you don't want it! Some of the results that may come from doing this are divorce and broken homes, just to name a few.

December 16, 2011

Relationships God's way: So, how do you do this?

1) Do you want the marriage that God has for you?

2) How do you know who is the one for you?

These are a few of the topics that will be addressed as we journey through Season of Preparation.

Well, first of all, you must be willing to do things God's way.

You may be asking yourself, what is God's way? (He knows the plans He has for you. Oh yeah, right, He does). SR: Jeremiah 29:11

<u>So, how do you do this?</u>

1) Be willing to ask Him to guide you in your relationships with single men and women who you are interested in, even your close friendships.

So, why is this important? In my opinion from experiences of myself and many others, it is easy to get caught up, and seek commitment in situations that are not led by God.

2) Be willing to become the person who you want to marry—Yes, I said it.

Check under your "personal hood" (like the hood of a car) and see what is actually there. There will be some "good stuff," but there will also be some "not-so-good" stuff there. Check yourself!

3) Seek to understand the roles of marriage (husband/wife).

Have you truly sought God and godly mentors on what it means to be a husband or a wife?

Lesson Learned
Check under your "personal hood" and see what is actually there.

Have you truly sought to get knowledge, wisdom, and understanding on what a godly/healthy marriage looks like? SR: Ephesians 5:22–33

~~~~~~~~~~~~~~~~~~~~~~~~~~~~

Have we allowed what others have experienced to taint our belief that God has a blessed marriage for us?

Biblical marriage is a picture of Christ's love and relationship with His beloved bride, the church.

T-Time

My testimony

As a single Christian woman, getting to a place of understanding biblical marriage has been somewhat overwhelming, with good and not-so-good experiences.

I made a decision to surrender my life to Jesus Christ as Lord and Savior in 2001, and immediately my life did a "180 degree" change.

It was one change, after another change ...my life was turned completely inside out!

Something that we are often not taught when we become Christians is how to "live out" Christianity. As new believers in Christ, we must learn how to undo a lot of what we've done and believed for many years prior to becoming a Christian.

Yes, I wanted to do the right thing, be a good Christian woman, and live how I was supposed to live. I did not know how to do it initially—things were really hard.

The things from your past do not just go away. It is usually in your relationships where everything is tested. It is in your relationships where you have to rely on God's help to interact with and respond to others in the ways that produce successful outcomes.

Lesson Learned
As new believers in Christ, we must learn how to undo a lot of what we've done and believed for many years prior to becoming a Christian.

So, what about having sex outside of the marriage?

My new lifestyle as a single Christian woman of no sex outside of marriage (celibacy) was rejected by my then fiancé. I soon learned that this lifestyle was respected yet, rejected as well by most other men who I have encountered along this journey. My new lifestyle was leading me to choose to not have pre-marital sex, changing something that had been an important part of my relationships.

I struggled with my own desires and wanted things to go back to the way they were, but I was in love with Jesus now. He loves me more than any man could!

Yes, that is right, but the struggle is real! I struggled with accepting my new life, the new person I had become, and I felt like no one understood what was really happening to me.

I couldn't explain it because I didn't fully understand what was happening myself.

3

Prayers for the Journey

What a friend we have in Jesus...

What a friend we have in Jesus—He beared all of our sins and grievances; what a privilege to carry...everything to God in prayer!

A very important component of Season of Preparation is prayer.

Prayer is key during the Season of Preparation! God will never leave you nor will He forsake you, regardless of how your circumstances may cause you to question or doubt. SR: Deuteronomy 31:6.

Ladies! Yes, you are Marriage Material! The right man from the Lord will recognize you as you continue to prepare and grow up...growing up to the standards you must have in order to show Him (your future spouse) and the rest of the world, who you are!

Lesson Learned
What a privilege to carry everything to God in prayer!

What is prayer?

Prayer is an intimate expression of our faith and trust in God. Sometimes you may need others to intercede for you in areas where you need to be strengthened. As I seek to do the "Will of God," I do not have it all together and I must trust in the guidance and leading of God.

I have longed to have someone care about my marriage and pray for me and with me during this season of my life. We pray for others when they are sick, in need of financial provision or going through more serious family issues, etc. I have not heard many prayer requests where we are praying for single adults to be strengthened on their journey to the marriage that God has for them.

A shout out to my single sisters: Watch Out! Here comes Mr. Right (or Wrong).

Please pray without ceasing. Pray...pray...pray and pray some more! SR: 1 Thessalonians 5:17

Prayer #1

Prayer areas:

1) <u>There is power in being a praying wife</u>

Reality check

Reality is that your husband or wife will not be perfect. Your spouse may hurt your feelings, be inconsiderate, uncaring, abusive, irritating, and negligent.

Ladies, when you are married, you are your husband's wife. The more you cover him in prayer, the more you are covered and protected by prayer!

This principle is not gender specific and can be applied to gentlemen as well. I encourage single men to pray for their future wives as well.

2) <u>Pray for God to remove ungodly attitudes</u>

Examples: Resentment, anger, unforgivingness, and so on.

Lord, please mow the grass of my heart...removing weeds and shaping my heart in the way you would have for it to be.

3) <u>Pray to keep sin out</u>

Why is it so important for us not to sin? What is sin? God knows we are all going to sin, right? SR: Romans 3:23

Where are you in different areas of sin in your life? God knows all things, but He gives us choices...we have free will.

<u>Questions that will help you address sin in your life</u>

Oftentimes, we want to point out the sin in other people's lives and do not address our own sins.

1. What areas of sin are you justifying in your mind?

2. Would God be pleased by your activities or your thoughts, even if they only involve you?

3. What do you do when you fall head over heels into sin?

Lesson Learned
God knows all things, but He gives us choices…we have free will.

SR: Genesis 4:7 states that sin crouches at the door of you life and desires to overtake you. We must make a conscious effort to rule over the sins that come up in our lives.

We are not to be slaves to sin, but to honor God with our bodies. SR: 1 Corinthians 6:19–20.

If not dealt with, those private actions or thoughts (still sin) will start to rear their ugly heads during the most inopportune times.

You may desire to be married, but if you do not deal with those things now (you know what they are), these same things will follow you into your "marriage" and have a negative impact on your relationship with your spouse.

SR: Hebrews 13:4 states that marriage should be honored by all, and the marriage bed kept pure.

There are so many times that I have said, "Well, at least I am not doing _____". Now, fill in the blank with the sins that you condemn others for doing, yet ignore the sins that you commit.

Based on what I know sin to be and that God hates sin, justifying or making excuses for my sin does not save me from God's judgment of sin.

Sin leaves the door open for the devil, and he comes to steal, kill, and to destroy. Sin is not to be entered into lightly and it does have consequences.

Do not allow justification of sin in your life lead you to destruction!

Always remember that God is faithful and forgives us of confessed sin and cleanses us of all unrighteousness. SR: 1 John 1:9

When we confess our sin, we come into agreement with God on what He says about sin in our lives.

Lord, I repent of _____ (list your sins) and will seek your power for inner strength to turn away from sin and not justify it.

Lesson Learned
When we confess sin, we come into agreement with God on what He says about sin in our lives.

My prayer

My Lord, please show me how to address any areas of public and private sin that I have in my life. Regardless of whether it is entertaining certain thoughts, contemplating specific activities, or engaging in certain actions, help me to see eye to eye with you on the issues at hand—Amen.

Prayer #2

Always pray—without ceasing. SR: 1 Thessalonians 5:17. Continue to pray during your Season of Preparation! Always pray in this place; pursuing God and responding to His pursuit of you.

SR: Psalm 25

1) A song/prayer for the single woman (or man)

Verse 14—The secret of the Lord is for those who fear Him, and He will make them know His covenant.

Verse 15—My eyes are continually toward the Lord, for He will pluck my feet out of the net.

Verse 16—Turn to me and be gracious to me, for I am lonely and afflicted.

Verse 17—The troubles of my heart are enlarged; bring me out of my distress.

Verse 18—Look upon my affliction and my trouble, and forgive all my sins.

Verse 19—Look upon my enemies, for they are many, and they hate me with a violent hatred.

Verse 20—Guard my soul.

Lesson Learned
Continue to pray during your Season of Preparation!

T-Time

There is one who comes to kill, steal, and destroy me (and you). SR: John 10:10.

He is our enemy (Satan), and he wants to influence you to be impatient and exclude the guidance of God from your journey toward marriage.

I have felt *afflicted, embarrassed, troubled, attacked,* and completely *distraught* at times along the journey of my Season of Preparation.

But, I have gained strength through growing my prayer life! I have learned that our God is greater! SR: 1 John 4:4 states that greater is the one who is in us than the one who is in this world.

2) <u>My personal prayer for my marriage</u>

Addressing physical attraction—just because you are physically attracted to someone, that does not mean you should marry them.

Lord, I pray that my husband and I will possess matching heart's desires for one another. I also pray that both of our heart's will chase after you and desire to live our lives in ways that are obedient to you. Lord, you do not focus on the outward appearance of man, but you place an emphasis on the heart.

SR: 1 Samuel 16:7

But the Lord said to Samuel, "Do not consider his appearance or his height, for I have rejected him. The Lord does not look at the things that man looks at. Man looks at the outward appearance, but the Lord looks at the heart."

More prayers

Lord, please show me my husband's heart for you. If I am to follow him, he must be following after you. He will wholeheartedly take your calling upon his life seriously and intentionally.

Lord, you are so faithful in all of your ways. I want to acknowledge you in every way, allowing you to direct my paths. I know that your plans are perfect, I know that your will is perfect and I know that your ways are perfect. Lord, please have your way in my heart.

December 21, 2011

God—our maker and our creator

God is our maker. It is not us who have created us, but he created us for his glory and to help make his name great in this earth. His love for us is an everlasting love and nothing or no one can compare to this great love.

SR: Isaiah 54:5

For thy Maker is thine husband; the Lord of hosts is his name; and thy Redeemer the Holy One of Israel; the God of the whole earth shall he be called.

SR: Isaiah 54:17

"No weapon that is formed against thee shall prosper; and every tongue that shall rise against thee in judgment thou shalt condemn. This is the heritage of the servants of the Lord, and their righteousness is of me," saith the Lord. Amen!

T-Time

My testimony

So, what does it mean when the scripture says that God or Jesus is your husband?

As women and men, oftentimes, we look at so many things and people to provide and be for us what only God is able to be for us. This is called idol worship. We must learn to allow God to be all and everything for us.

The way that I have been able to connect to the heart of God, who is my source, is through prayer.

This has happened through prayers of worship and petition to the Lord, but I have also learned to intercede on behalf of my fellow sisters and brothers.

Our hearts are sensitive, and sometimes only God can fill the spaces of hurt, confusion, and needed understanding/clarity that we have deep within our hearts.

I am so thankful to God for prayer…mere words cannot express my gratitude!

4

A Time for Everything

Time is always of the essence

It is a rare commodity, and oftentimes during the Season of Preparation, we say to God—"Are we there yet?"

SR: Ecclesiastes 3:1 "There is an appointed time for everything. And there is a time for every event under heaven."

Patience with God's timing must infiltrate every aspect of our lives!

<u>Remember</u>: He is the creator of all things and he is the creator of time.

Waiting on God's timing

<u>Points to remember</u>:

1. It is difficult to understand God's timing.

2. God's timing may seem really slow according to our standards of time.

3. God's timing can be swift at times…when it is time for something to happen, you know what…it happens suddenly!

We must go along with time. Once something happens, it happens, and we must be ready.

Sometimes we are left in a position with time where we do not have a choice in the effects and actions of time.

<u>A message on God's timing from the book of Esther</u>

The book of Esther is a story about a time when the people of God were saved through the obedient acts of Queen Esther and her uncle Mordecai. They both made decisions in the right time and God's people were saved as a result.

Queen Esther *fasted, prayed,* and *sought* the face of God for His direction and timing before she went to see the King, who was her husband. She wanted him to help to free her people (the Jews) from bondage.

This was an act of courage because Queen Esther could have lost her life for going before the King at the wrong time.

Queen Esther was aware of the plots and schemes against her people, God's people, and it was her turn to fulfill her assignment in helping them. She had to do what was necessary for God's people to be saved and delivered from the hands of their enemies.

SR: Esther 4:14 "For if you remain silent at this time, relief and deliverance will arise for the Jews from another place and you and your father's house will perish. And who knows whether you have not attained royalty for such a time as this?"

Where are you as it relates to God's timing?

A few questions to think on:

1. Do you get angry and impatient while waiting on God's timing?

2. Do you stay motivated when it seems like everything is taking too long?

3. Are there areas in your life where you can be more patient with God's timing?

Regardless of who you are, we all have room to practice patience in the area of waiting on God's timing.

Lesson Learned
...we all have room to practice patience in the area of waiting on God's timing.

My prayer for God's timing

Lord, I thank you and praise you for your timing. Your time is of the essence, and it is evident and clear that you are "in time and always on time."

Your Spirit operates in time, my Lord. We praise you and thank you for your presence and authority in time. You are sovereign, powerful and omnipresent. Please empower me to allow your Spirit to help me be more patient and trust in your timing.

T-Time

The "I want it right now" syndrome:

This syndrome can have some not-so-good implications in our circumstances and throughout our lives. Do not rush through things in your life, even during your Season of Preparation, that is leading you to your marriage.

Even as I write this book, I am fighting through the desires to rush God. I see so many situations where others have what I desire.

Lesson Learned
Do not rush through things in your life, even during your Season of Preparation, that is leading you to your marriage.

So why am I not there yet?

Oftentimes, others ask me questions like, "Why aren't you married yet?"

Well, this is the same question that I ask God in my private time.

The only answer that I get from God is that…

"It is not time for your marriage, but stay in faith, your time is coming."

Then there are others who say, "Don't rush being single…marriage is hard!"

I agree; and I have talked to enough people who are married or who have been married, to recognize that being married can be challenging.

~~~~~~~~~~~~~~~~~~~~~~~~~~~~~~

But, I have also seen many beautiful marriages as well,

and

I believe that God has a beautiful marriage for me.

~~~~~~~~~~~~~~~~~~~~~~~~~~~~~~

God has a beautiful marriage for those who are single. He also has a beautiful marriage for those who are currently married, but may be experiencing difficult times.

A marriage God's way is multifaceted and can have a much bigger impact than we could ever know.

Lesson Learned
A marriage God's way is multifaceted and can have a much bigger impact than we could ever know.

5

Faith to Believe

Now, faith is the substance of things hoped for…

T-Time

My testimony

Believing and having faith for my marriage has been one of the hardest things to do during this season of my life. There have been so many false starts: Is he the one…no, wrong guy, moments…that I have just wanted to give up and throw in the towel.

Always the bridesmaid, but not the bride…yet…

- I was engaged to be married;
- Believed the wrong men were my husband;
- Been pursued by men who thought I was their wives;

and the list goes on… But, I still have not made it to my marriage from God. Although these situations did not work out, I am good, and I am happy—I'd rather be married to the right man at the right time and be the right woman when I get there. These are factors that can make the marriage a better experience for me and my future spouse.

Lesson Learned
I'd rather be married to the right man at the right time and be the right woman when I get there.

Keeping the faith during your Season of Preparation!

Questions to ponder:

1. How is God growing your faith today?

2. What evidence of things not seen are you believing God for today?

3. Do you believe God is able to perform miracles for you and others today?

SR: Hebrews 11:1—Faith is the substance of things hoped for, the evidence of things not seen. Remember: Faith is required to please our Heavenly Father! SR: Hebrews 11:6

Some days…it is really hard for me to believe

There are some days when it is really hard to believe. Lord, I know that you are drawing me closer to you, but my heart aches—it hurts in the familiar place…where I know that I have to be intentional and not seek after any man or person to fill my life, but seek you.

Lesson Learned
Remember: Faith is required to please our Heavenly Father.

A message from the heart of God to me...
"A football analogy"

The football analogy that is used in this message is the "line of scrimmage".

This example maybe familiar to most men and also to some women. This familiar football term references the invisible line between two opposing teams that cannot be crossed until the football play has begun.

<u>What does it mean to stay behind the "line of scrimmage"?</u>

1) You must stay behind the "line of scrimmage" or you will be penalized.

2) Every time, you go "offside"—this means to cross too quickly over the "line of scrimmage", you were on the opposing team's side when the play began. This is a penalty.

During your Season of Preparation (SOP), this means to move ahead of God on the journey toward your marriage.

If you do this, you will be penalized right where it hurts—in your heart! You may be asking, "what does all of this mean"? What this essentially means is that God wants me (and you) to wait on Him before entering into a relationship. He wants me to seek Him before I let someone into that special place in my heart that is reserved especially for my spouse. Do not cross the "line of scrimmage" before the right time.

Lesson Learned
** What this essentially means is that God wants me (and you) to wait on Him before entering into a relationship.**

T-Time

My testimony

In this place, during my Season of Preparation…

I have had feelings of…

~~~~~~~~~~~~~~~~~~~~~~~~~~

> **Pain**
> (*from dealing with unfulfilled desires and unsuccessful relationships*)
>
> **Embarrassment**
> (*from not having a man, or desiring someone who does not feel the same way about me*)
>
> **Uneasiness**
> (*in the relationship that I may have been in*)
>
> **Fear**
> (*of not getting what I feel God has promised me, or what I want*)
>
> And simply put…..
>
> **Anger & Annoyance!**

~~~~~~~~~~~~~~~~~~~~~~~~~~

Dealing with your emotions

This testimony is from a time when my emotions were trying to overwhelm me, but after spending time with God and seeking Him through prayer, a breakthrough was released!

Be honest and truthful with yourself.

Honesty is the best policy!

The fact is that emotions can come up and try to take over your life at times. Some days, it is hard for me to hide them. This can really be challenging on days when there are no friends available to talk to…no activities…and nothing to do that can cover things up.

My heart is crying out to God…

- Lord, it is just me and you today, and you know what…I am listening to some worship music, which is taking my focus off me and what I want, and I am placing my focus on you as the one who will be with me always.

- Lord, I know that you want me to love you more than anything or anyone, and I am going to be okay today.

I may have to cry…

I may be a little sad and feel disappointed…

but you are so faithful Lord.

I cannot place so much emphasis on this area of my life, and my heart being occupied by a man. God, you are enough for me!

The breakthrough

Whew…the more I press into this place with you Lord, the better I feel! I can truly be honest with you and let you know where my heart is.

You are not going to dislike me or be offended by my honesty.

Thank you for accepting me Lord, even when I say things that may not seem spiritual, or act in ways that are not pleasing to you.

I praise your name, my Lord!

What should you do when it is hard to believe?

1. Focus on God and not on the circumstances…

   You may be wondering…why am I not married yet? Well, I have wondered this on numerous occasions, but once I placed my focus on God, I found the peace needed to keep moving forward in my purpose.

2. Praise the Lord and lift up His name…

   Something that has worked for me is playing uplifting praise music!

3. Pour your heart out to God, and if necessary, cry…

4. Wait on the Lord to inhabit your life…He inhabits the praises of His people. SR: Psalm 22:3

> 5. Remember God's promises, such as, SR: Psalm 37:4, or any other promises that you have claimed from God's word.

Whenever your faith wavers and things get difficult, you have to be intentional to not remain there. You want to draw near to God, so that He will draw near to you. SR: James 4:8

Do not allow the enemy to steal your joy and keep you in a place where you are feeling sad regarding circumstances that are beyond your control. Always remember, you are okay, even if you do not have a significant other or a spouse right now!

~~~~~~~~~~~~~~~~~~~~~~~~~~~~~~~~~~~~

Lesson Learned
Always remember, you are okay, even if you do not have a significant other or a spouse right now!

December 22, 2011

Just Believe!

Believe God and follow after Him!

I am not sure of what all God has told you, but *believe*.

The odds may be stacked miles high against you…but just *believe.*

Why is faith in God necessary?

Faith is the evidence of things not seen…SR: Hebrews 11:1

If everything always made sense and was laid out before us, faith in God would not be needed…just *believe*!

No matter what…no matter when…no matter how…or for how long…leave the details up to God, just *believe*!

He is pleased by our faith in Him, just *believe*…SR: Hebrews 11:6

Then, watch the windows of heaven open up…and pour out your specific blessings…more than you could imagine or hope for!
SR: Ephesians 3:20–21

JUST BELIEVE!

6

Dealing with You

Before you focus on what is wrong with others, you must deal with you first...

T-Time

My testimony

I have learned many valuable lessons during my Season of Preparation. One thing that I have learned is that the person you are while single, is the same person who you will be once you get married.

There isn't some "magic spell" that is broken once you become a married person.

If you do not deal with you and your issues now (in your current life season), when will you deal with them?

I have spent a lot of time dealing with me, different parts, in different ways, and there are more layers of me that I need to work through.

My advice is this…

When something comes up, deal with it! Deal with you! Your future spouse will greatly appreciate it!

Lesson Learned
When something comes up, deal with it! Deal with you!

Take some time to get to know you!

<u>Some questions to consider are…</u>

1. What is your true identity?

    Who do you say that you are? Who does God say that you are?

2. What is your purpose?

    What were you created to do? Are you giving back and sowing seeds of your time and finances into the lives of other people?

3. Who are you when no one is there to impress?

    Who are you when no one else is looking at you?

4. What are the things that get a reaction out of you and make you tick?

    What are your fears, concerns, and things that make you angry?

Knowing the answers to these questions and many more can be a tremendous help, and have a huge impact on your personal and professional relationships.

These answers can drive how we treat ourselves and can help us to have more effective and healthier relationships with others.

More questions to consider

1. How well do you know yourself?

    This is a relevant question…

    "Although I have known myself for many years, I still surprise myself from time to time…"

    There is also value in asking close friends and family members their opinion on certain areas of your personality.

    This will help you to see if you are portraying the self-image that you want others to see from you.

2. Are you a good friend?

    What makes you a good friend? How can you be a better friend to others?

3. Do you make wise decisions?

    How do you make decisions? What are some wise choices that you have made?

4. Do you have a positive work ethic?

   Are you dependable and punctual with your responsibilities?

5. Do you have a good attitude most of the time?

6. How do you feel about your life's accomplishments?

7. What are some areas of insecurity in your life?

8. What areas are you confident about in your life?

This list is an example, but there are many more questions that you can add to the list.

Take an assessment of your important life areas

Important points to ponder

1) Spiritual/family/personal

As people, we are spiritual beings and all areas of our lives are influenced by the fact that we were born into sin. There is no point in pretending that you do not sin and that this is not a problem. This fact impacts us spiritually, in our families and on a personal level. We must be sensitive to the specific areas where we struggle with all sin. As we do this, we can allow God to intervene and help us when our actions lean into that direction.

How do you react when you are lonely, tired, hungry, angry, or when your feelings are hurt?

These are all areas to look at because they all have the potential to impact our relationships, and if there are improper reactions, they can negatively impact your future marriage. SR: Romans 3:23

2) Career/ministry/business

Are you moving forward in these areas? What are the challenges?

Are there areas of needed development, training, or education that you need?

Are you angry, bitter, disappointed, or in an undesirable place in your career/ministry/business?

There are many resources available that can assist you on this journey. Getting clarity in these areas will help you in achieving your life goals.

3) Purpose/ life fulfillment

Are you taking the necessary steps to fulfill your life purpose? Do you know your purpose?

Do you have a plan in place to help you move forward into your life purpose?

Are you truly fulfilled in your life? Do you feel like something is missing?

Be true to yourself and seek to be who you really are everyday!

T-Time

My testimony

During my Season of Preparation I have not always been comfortable being Jacole at times. I became somewhat insecure with the lifestyle changes that I experienced as a Christian. I wanted to live a life that was pleasing to God, and this decision brought about many changes.

I learned quickly that being a person who truly believes that he or she should live by the principles of the Bible may not be easy to do. I also learned that this does not always make you the most popular person in the world.

The Bible says that believers were left in the world by God, but are not of this world. SR: John 17:15–16

This means that you may not always fit in with others, which can be challenging to your relationships.

Do not compromise yourself: No means, no!

As you are on this journey, it is so tempting to do things that compromise your core beliefs and move away from who you really are.

Compromise comes in all shades, flavors, and areas throughout our lives. Whenever you start to second-guess yourself, or feel a sense of not being true to yourself or not following the directions that you have received from God, you are in danger of compromise. It is always good at this point, to slow down, so that you can really assess what is going on.

If God says no, or your inner self says no, don't compromise! Yes, compromise is tempting, and may seem right in the eyes of man, but in the end, it leads to destruction…your destruction…moving you away from your purpose…moving you into unhealthy relationships, bad decisions…and the list goes on…SR: Proverbs 14:12

Lesson Learned
Do not compromise yourself: No means, no!

A couple years ago, I received the message "Don't compromise"! I did not understand why I was being told this since I was not living a compromising lifestyle, but was seeking to follow God daily.

After reflecting on this more, I realized that I had an issue with acceptance. This issue made it tempting for me to compromise my true self in different ways. What I have learned was that the real issue was me accepting myself, not someone else accepting me.

The man who God has for you will accept you, and all you have to do is, be yourself. The more confident you become in who you are, others will accept you, because you are truly being who God created you to be.

Be true to yourself when…

1) Making important decisions:

When you are in the process of making decisions/investments, it is so important to be true to yourself!

This has been a very important place of realization on my journey of living out my purpose.

2) Living out your purpose daily:

Declare positive things over your life

- You are important.
- Your thoughts and desires are relevant.
- Your contributions are meaningful.

Your life's investment will impact your future and the future of those connected to you in life. You never know how others can become better and be inspired to live out their purpose, simply by something that you say or do.

Dealing with you: From the inside/out

A large part of accepting yourself is seeing your true beauty. We are beautiful, and this is best seen when we are not focusing on what we do not have, but focusing on what we actually have.

Instead of being so preoccupied with what you are wearing on the outside, focus more on being the person God created you to be, and being the best you every day. This is not an excuse to neglect your appearance and not take care of yourself.

SR: 1 Peter 3:3–4

1 Peter 3:3: Your beauty should not come from outward adornment,

such as elaborate hairstyles and the wearing of gold jewelry or fine clothes.

1 Peter 3:4: Rather, it should be that of your inner self, the unfading beauty of a gentle and quiet spirit, which is of great worth in God's sight.

God values you totally—inside and outside. Although we tend to focus more on the outside appearance of things, God cares deeply about you and what is going on inside of you as well! SR: 1 Peter 5:7

God cares when your feelings are hurt and He cares when you are disappointed—He cares when you are in pain, sad, happy, and even confused.

God cares about you, Period! Always remember that!

Lesson Learned
God cares about you, Period! Always remember that!

Heart health: Do you have a healthy heart?

Heart health is oftentimes associated with your physical health. This concept is not frequently used to speak about the condition of your heart with regards to areas surrounding love and relationships.

How many of you know that relationships can impact your entire life—emotionally, physically, psychologically, and so on?

Some questions for us to ponder:

1. Has your heart ever been broken?

2. How many times has your heart been broken by someone you love and care about?

3. What do you usually do when your heart is broken?

This list can go on and on. The main point that I am making is to ask yourself questions that cause you to look at the current and past life events that have caused a negative impact on your heart.

How does the health of your heart impact other people (loved ones, children, and so on)?

A fact that we have all experienced in our lives at some point in time is that hurt people hurt other people.

Most hurtful things in life do not just go away. They must be addressed and dealt with. If we choose to not deal with them, negative patterns may manifest through our lives in personal and professional relationships.

Lesson Learned
A fact that we have all experienced in our lives at some point in time is that hurt people hurt other people.

Let's take a look at some signs of a healthy heart versus an unhealthy heart:

<u>A healthy heart</u>:

- Loving
- Kind
- Faithful
- Giving
- Life speaking
- Joyous
- Patient

<u>An unhealthy heart</u>:

- Unforgivingness
- Easily find fault in others
- Anger
- Depression
- Unfaithful
- Argumentative
- Taking advantage of others

Let's take a journey toward a healthier heart

In order to change anything in your life, you must first acknowledge that you have an issue. You must have a desire to change in order to experience true change.

My encouragement for you is to embark upon this journey of looking into your heart. Take some time to really see what's there. Once you see what's there, come up with a plan to address any issues that you find. Some of the symptoms may have been there for years, but just because they have been there, that doesn't mean they are supposed to stay there.

<u>It is eviction time!</u>

Be intentional and get those unhealthy habits, patterns and emotions out of your heart. Your heart health and the heart health of those who you are connected to depends on it!

~~~~~~~~~~~~~~~~~~~~~~~~~~~~

7

Be Healed

Our God is a healer…

T-Time

My testimony

There are things in life that we all may have experienced, that have left you puzzled, confused, perplexed and with a "hole" in your heart.

Although it may seem easier to ignore these issues and cover them up with make-up, new relationships, and so on, until the "hole" in your heart is addressed, the more the confusion will continue.

Despite any past hurt or pain that you may have experienced, always remember, there is healing in our Lord!

~~~~~~~~~~~~~~~~~~~~~~

Dealing with matters/issues of the heart:

Oh, my Lord, how excellent are you in all the earth!

"The earth is the Lord's and the fullness thereof…" SR: Psalm 24:1

When looking at the matters of the heart, and issues that lie within our hearts, most issues are usually magnified through relationships.

As we interact with others in close proximity, we can see our flaws, and so can they.

Well, since there are no perfect people, what do we do about this?

When I look at some of my relationships and some of the internal conflicts that I experience at times, I have to take a couple steps back and ask myself—what in the world is going on here? Oh my goodness, things can really get a little crazy and confusing—LOL!

I am so grateful for your grace, Lord! Your grace is sufficient and it covers a multitude of sins! SR: 1 Peter 4:8

Dealing with the past

Another key component to consider during your Season of Preparation is realizing and knowing where you have come from. Everyone came from somewhere, and everyone has a past.

There are many ways that your past has impacted who you are, where you are, and what has become of your life.

Whether these experiences are positive, negative, or neutral, they have all impacted your life in some way or another.

How do you feel when you look at your past? Do you feel happy, sad, emotional, or distressed?

The experiences of others have also impacted your life. The choices and decisions that your parents or ancestors made have definitely impacted your life and who you are.

So, how do you deal with the past?

We have to sometimes take a deep and introspective look and make a list of what should stay in our lives and what needs to be thrown out.

Why do you do what you do? Do you know what factors drive a particular behavior that you possess?

There are so many things that happen throughout our lives, and we rarely stop to figure out why the specific negative behaviors are there. Before we know it, our children exhibit the same negative behaviors…they become victims of the generational transfer in the same way the negative behaviors were transferred to us.

The awesome point in this message is that God gives us deliverance and healing from our past issues. God is able to "break negative behavior cycles" in our lives if we allow Him to do so. Deliverance is real and God can do it for you!

Our past contains memories and our human nature may lean into the direction of those memories. Before we know it, our past is active and alive in our current circumstances, and seeking to live in your future.

Lesson Learned
God is able to "break negative behavior cycles" in our lives if we allow Him to do so.

So, when the past resurfaces, how do you deal with it? Do you want it to remain in your current circumstances, impacting future generations in your family?

Do you want these negative behavior cycles to stop with you?

History lessons: Taking a journey through your life

Something else that I have found to be very important is being determined and doing what it takes to move forward.

In order to do this, you must identify the things from your past and present that keep popping up in your life to hold you back, impacting your future progress. These things not only impact you but they also can impact your future mate and they can impact your children.

How do you do this effectively? (The process)

A way to begin this process is to take a look at all that is on the inside of you. This is something that only you and God can do. You must be committed to the process in order for it to accomplish the best results.

Although this can be a little challenging, taking a tour of the inside of you can prove to be very beneficial for your life!

<u>A way to begin this process is to look at</u> :
"Why do you do what you do?"

1. Develop a list of the specific details of the behaviors that you are concerned about.

2. Develop a list of specific areas that you would like to pray about.

3. Keep going through this process, be determined, and do not give up!

<u>This is not a quick process; it requires commitment!</u>

This process is necessary to experience freedom from your past. Even if you do not follow the exact steps listed, please follow another process that will help you to address issues from your past. These areas may have to be revisited at different times throughout your life.

Complete deliverance and healing is optional, and many do not commit to the process.

Something to remember, however, is the more you prolong this process, choosing not to deal with your past, the more these issues will keep you from moving forward in your life.

Seek God for his help! SR: Psalm 121:2

Ask God what areas He wants you to address, and allow Him to lead you to complete deliverance and healing!

Addressing unhealthy relationship connections

There are many television shows and media communications about toxic relationships.

There seems to be more information out here that focus on unhealthy relationships than on having healthy relationships.

Learning to deal with unhealthy relationship connections, whatever they are, is something that we must do. Unhealthy relationship connections can be difficult to break free from, because our human nature has gotten used to them, and they have become a part of our comfort zones.

An interesting point that I have observed from conversations with many different people, is that people associate negative issues with relationships more than they associate positive situations. Some of the negative issues that are associated with relationships range from infidelity/cheating, abuse, wrong attitudes and divorce—versus more positive situations such as fidelity/faithfulness, unconditional love and support.

Unhealthy connections can be a person, place, job, or wherever you may find yourself. They can also be a mind-set, a personality trait, or even an unhealthy connection through a habit that you may have.

Despite the type of connections or relationships that you may have in your life, it is always more beneficial to focus on having healthy connections and relationships.

Unhealthy connections are not worth wasting your time, energy, and life on!

<u>Let's deal with unhealthy connections with people</u>

Ladies (and gentlemen), let's be real with ourselves.

As I have been on the journey through my Season of Preparation, I have learned to be more conscious of who I am connected to.

I have learned to ask myself questions, such as:

Why am I in this person's life? Should I remain in their life and should they remain in my life? Is this a mutual relationship?

Lesson Learned
Unhealthy connections are not worth wasting your time, energy, and life on!

So, let's take a look at where you are now...

1. Is your relationship connection healthy or unhealthy?

2. Should this man or woman remain in your life?

3. How does this connection make you feel?

4. Is this connection encouraging and positive?

After completing this evaluation, what if you realize that your relationship connection is unhealthy?

More questions

1) How can you disconnect from this relationship?

2) What should this connection be replaced with?

Do not replace the relationship with the same type of relationship!

Sometimes the real issue is not the person who you are involved with; sometimes the real issue is with you.

3) Do you need to reclassify your definition of healthy relationships?

As a result of us being a part of unhealthy relationships, we become accustomed to the patterns of unhealthy relationships. To correct the wrong patterns, we must completely redefine what a healthy relationship is.

If you are having a difficult time with this, pray and seek God on what this should look like for your life.

The bottom line is, when it comes to unhealthy relationship connections, cut them out of your life!

Disconnect from the unhealthy relationship, cold turkey!

As people, a lot of times, we try to fill voids in our lives with people, but only God can truly fill these voids!

During my Season of Preparation, I have also learned that the best replacement for unhealthy relationship connections in my life is spending more time with God. I also learned to spend time with friends, spend time with family members, and to invest more time into me.

We experience more damage in our lives by trying to hold on to things and people that God wants us to let go of. Letting go of that unhealthy relationship may be painful at first, but the benefits are great in the end.

Lesson Learned
As people, a lot of times, we try to fill voids in our lives with people, but only God can truly fill these voids!

8

Lifting Up the Father

Exalt His name and lift Him up…

T-Time

My testimony

To the detriment of my relationship with you (Lord)….

In the process of dealing with the desire for marriage, some of my actions have been to the detriment of my relationship with you (Lord).

The area that I am most likely to take God out of His rightful position in my life is in my relationship with another man…Oh, Lord, how we put earthly men before you…There are times that I have been tempted, and at other times I have fallen into some type of sin (lust/temptations). This happened because I put my desire to be in the attention and affection of an earthly man above you Lord.

Not that this desire is wrong or unnatural, but never to the detriment of my relationship with you …. Oh Lord, the things we do, to the detriment of our relationship with you. My Lord, I am in an interesting place and I really desire to see your mighty hand move in my marriage.

Although there have been some struggles, I have always been in a place of submission to you as it relates to my desire for marriage. I have also desired to be in a place of honoring my relationship with you, Lord.

I thank and praise you for keeping me, even when I don't want to be kept—thanks for keeping, guiding, and protecting me, my Lord!

What are you offering God today?

Are you offering God the best (choice) time of your day, or are you offering the leftover time that He really cannot work with because you are tired.

Now, think about it, do you want a "choice time" blessing from God, or do you want a leftover blessing from God?

This message speaks to the quality of our relationship with Christ and the time that we spend in prayer, praise, and reading God's word.

Oftentimes, we do not put what we should put into this relationship, yet, we expect miraculous blessings from God.

Even though we may need to do some work in the area of spending time with Him, God still provides for us and meets our needs.

He is so faithful! This point validates why we should always praise Him!

So, do not spend time with God out of an obligation, but spend time with Him as an expression of your appreciation and love for Him. Offer to the Lord more of your time…

Lesson Learned
** He is so faithful! This point validates why we should always praise Him!**

T-Time

My testimony

As God moves and blesses me…

My week has been very interesting, Lord, and things just keep getting more interesting.

But as you move, you bless me in such profound ways!

I want to change my focus and shift it more to you…and what you would like to happen in my life in this moment! Lord, I want to stop attempting to get you to do what I want you to do.

As you are training me up in the way that I should go, I know that I will not always agree with you. (LOL—No, I do not always agree with God's ways… do you?)

I don't always enjoy this process, but you are so faithful to me Lord! Thank you, my Lord Jesus!

You know how to get me back into line with you. Your will always works best! When it is all said and done, God's will feels comfortable, and it works. We have all experienced times in our lives that feel great and things really work out.

Not my will Father, but thy will be done! SR: Luke 22:42

Submitting my heart to you, Lord

Who holds the true position of Lord in your life? Who guides the decisions that you make? Who do you ultimately seek for direction in your life?

Oh my Lord, how wonderful you are to me! How gracious and merciful you are to me!

There is no one like you in this earth! And the earth is yours and the fullness thereof…

This includes me—Yes, I said Me. I belong to you Lord.

I must pour my heart out before you daily, Lord, and allow you to search it. SR: Psalm 139:23

T-Time

My testimony

My desire for the marriage that God has for me and the journey that I have been on to get there, has taken a while and a lot has happened deep within me. I have longed for that person to be in my life since I was nineteen years old. Yes, it truly has been a long time …

Lord, I am tired of fighting and going through the challenges of this journey, but I know that this is necessary for me to fulfill my purpose in you.

I praise you for your protection, covering, and keeping me throughout this process and stopping me every time that have I tried to fit the "wrong man" into the place in my life that you created specifically for my mate/spouse/husband.

The "wrong man" may not be a disrespectful heathen…He can actually be a nice gentleman, hard worker, loving, and powerful man of God.

Just because I see these things in a man, that does not mean that I should put him in the place within my life that only God can fill—this is the place where my future spouse belongs.

1) How have you done this?

2) What should your criteria be?

3) How have you included God in your mate selection process?

4) Have you experienced pain and disappointment while waiting for your mate?

I have determined that there was one root cause to most of my pain, discomfort, and issues during my Season of Preparation.

Most of it was due to me trying to fulfill the desire to be married in my own strength and not totally relying upon God. Despite all of my experiences, there is no way for me to be fully equipped to do this apart from God.

Lord, you are the only man I want to trust and love.

God's plans are different for everyone. You can learn things from others, but you should not try and imitate all that they do. We can oftentimes focus on others, comparing our lives and our process to theirs. I could go on and on with this point, but I will stop here.

It is so easy for us to get off-track, and to see things different from how you want us to look at things, Lord...

October 26, 2012

Lord, I want to be where you are

Friday, October 26, 2012,—6:31 p.m.

Lord, I want to be where you are…and not caught up in the nonsense that I can so often get caught up in.

There is nothing wrong with the fun and exciting things of life, but sometimes, I need to have some time alone.

I am so glad that you have brought me to this place on a Friday evening. I am so accustomed to my Friday nights being filled with activities, and really, it is time out for being busy all the time.

Instead, I need to focus on the business that God has entrusted to me, which is to live out my life in purpose every day.

How can I really hear what I am supposed to do if I do not spend time with you and seek to be where you are, Lord?

Why am I tripping? Because I am not able to occupy my time with phone calls, text messages, or other activities…

These things are all well and fine, but I should not be tripping about this today…of all days…

When I am where you are, Lord, there is love, joy, peace that surpasses understanding…these are all here in your presence, Lord.

9

Getting ready for Marriage

He who finds a wife .....

T-Time

My testimony

As I have been on my Season of Preparation journey, waiting on Mr. Right to find me was really difficult at first, but things have progressively gotten better over time. I have dated the wrong man several times, but not Mr. Right as of yet. I have talked to several single men and women who have shared their frustrations and challenges about their journeys as well. What I have learned is when the right time comes, it happens!

I have known many people who have been successful in finding their mate. A common thought that many have shared is that preparation is important and that marriage is not a fairytale. The more you develop personally and grow in your relationship with God, the more you will be ready for the marriage that God has for you.

He who finds a wife

SR: Proverbs 18:22 states that he who finds a wife finds a good thing and receives favor from the Lord.

Making the decision on who you will marry is one of the most important life decisions that you will ever make.

Based on what this scripture says, there is favor and blessings on the man who finds his wife and that a wife is a good thing.

So, why does the journey of getting married take so long? Why do so many married people want to get out of marriage and divorce one another?

I do not know the answers to these questions, but what I have learned is that marriage is a beneficial yet sacrificial relationship. Many married people have shared with me that marriage is a very unselfish decision and that you want to make sure that you choose the right person.

Lesson Learned
**Making the decision on who you will marry is one of the most important life decisions that you will ever make. **

The two shall become one

SR: Matthew 19:25 states: For this reason a man will leave his father and mother and be united to his wife, and the two will become one flesh.

Based on this scripture, a man and a woman become one flesh within marriage. Since people are different, how is this accomplished? I have spoken with several married couples and most share that becoming one takes time, being considerate of one another, open communication, transparency and a lot of patience. It also requires genuine friendship and spouses who are truly willing to get to know one another. In order to get ready to participate in this process, it may be helpful to practice developing patience and being considerate of others in your life prior to marriage.

The process of consideration

In the process of considering someone to move forward in a committed relationship with, there are some important points that you may want to keep in mind. These are points to be mindful of during your single season, whether you are actively dating someone or not at the time.

Do not put yourself on hold and neglect the preparation process because God can bring your spouse when you least expect it.

When someone comes along...

1) Take the time to examine him/her.

   Do not jump into something just because it feels right.

2) Seek God daily on your interactions with this man/woman.

   This can be time consuming but definitely worthwhile.

3) Be open and honest about how you truly feel about different aspects of this person.

   Please be mindful that just because you do not like a particular thing about this man/woman, that does not mean that God will tell you to walk away from them.

4) Apply the lessons that you have learned.

   Apply the lessons learned from your own experiences and from experiences of others.

5) Relax —enjoy yourself and have fun! I believe that God wants us to enjoy things within the boundaries that He sets.

   If you have difficulty doing this, pray and seek God's face on how to do this.

Keeping hope alive ...

Every person who you date along your journey toward the marriage that God has for you will not be your spouse.

It can be difficult when things do not work out as planned, but it is better to know that prior to marriage.

When you are in a relationship, it is always good to keep the lines of communication open and to ask questions. You may be surprised by some of the things that you find out while asking the right questions. It may not always be comfortable to ask questions, but that should be one of the main objectives of the dating process.

Hope deferred makes the heart sick, but a longing fulfilled is a tree of life. SR: Proverbs 13:12

Continue to be hopeful, even when things do not work out the way that you desired.

You are complete without having a significant other in your life. The person who God has for you will only enhance your life, not complete you. God is our true provider and our source—He makes us complete.

Try to keep the right perspective as you are getting to know the man or woman that you are considering.

Lesson Learned
** God is our true provider and our source—He makes us complete.**

T-Time

My testimony

I have encountered some wonderful men along this journey. Sometimes, the people who cross our pathways are supposed to only be friends. When we try to make the relationship develop outside of the friendship boundaries, we can miss some great opportunities to build partnerships with people who may add value to our lives.

Learning how to let God lead in this process takes time, but developing healthy friendships with people of the opposite-sex can also be a helpful skill to have once you enter into marriage. Healthy relationships and partnerships are very important in all areas of our lives.

Making it to the finish line ...

Oftentimes, we are laser-focused on getting to the finish line, crossing it and obtaining the prize!

~~~~~~~~~~~~~~~~~~~~~~~~~~~~~~~~~~~

Lord, I am in a place of prayer and hope. I know that you have me and that I must trust and depend on you in this place....

I am a little panicky yet cautious— I want to get married but I will not settle for less than your best.

Just because someone approaches me, expresses an interest and thinks I am beautiful (inside and outside), that does not mean that I can allow the space reserved for my spouse to be filled by them.

Oftentimes, I ask others how they knew when their mate came along. To be honest, many of them sound as confused as I feel about this process. I believe that ultimately, none of us truly know initially. As we follow God, He confirms whether we are with the right person or not.

Most couples with wonderful marriages who I know have all gone through circumstances that caused them to wonder and have doubts about their marriages.

The place where I am is no different, except it is just occurring prior to my marriage relationship.

Oh Lord, I am seeking you to help me as I continue through this journey of my Season of Preparation!

10

References

Scripture reference (SR) list

All scriptures are from the New International Version

~~~~~~~~~~~~~~~~~~~~~~~~~~~~~~~~

1) Proverbs 3:5 – pg. 8
Trust in the Lord with all your heart and lean not on your own understanding;

2) Isaiah 55:8 – pg. 8
"For my thoughts are not your thoughts, neither are your ways my ways," declares the Lord.

3) Jeremiah 29:11 – pgs. 9, 24
For I know the plans I have for you, declares the Lord, plans to prosper you and not to harm you, plans to give you hope and a future.

4) Isaiah 54:17 – pgs. 20, 21, 23, 35 – 36
"No weapon forged against you will prevail, and you will refute every tongue that accuses you. This is the heritage of the servants of the LORD, and this is their vindication from me," declares the LORD.

5) Ephesians 6:12 – pg. 20
For our struggle is not against flesh and blood, but against the rulers, against the authorities, against the powers of this dark world and against the spiritual forces of evil in the heavenly realms.

6) Psalm 37:4 – pgs. 24, 48
Take delight in the Lord, and he will give you the desires of your heart.

7) Ephesians 5:22 – 33 – pg. 25
Wives, submit yourselves to your own husbands as you do to the Lord. [23] For the husband is the head of the wife as Christ is the head of the church, his body, of which he is the Savior. [24] Now as the church submits to Christ, so also wives should submit to their husbands in everything. [25] Husbands, love your wives, just as Christ loved the church and gave himself up for her [26] to make her holy, cleansing her by the washing with water through the word, [27] and to present her to himself as a radiant church, without stain or wrinkle or any other blemish, but holy and blameless. [28] In this same way, husbands ought to love their wives as their own bodies. He who loves his wife loves himself. [29] After all, no one ever hated their own body, but they feed and care for their body, just as Christ does the church—[30] for we are members of his body.[31] "For this reason

Season of Preparation 87

a man will leave his father and mother and be united to his wife, and the two will become one flesh." [32] This is a profound mystery—but I am talking about Christ and the church.[33] However, each one of you also must love his wife as he loves himself, and the wife must respect her husband.

8) Deuteronomy 31:6 – pg. 28
Be strong and courageous. Do not be afraid or terrified because of them, for the LORD your God goes with you; he will never leave you nor forsake you.

9) 1 Thessalonians 5:17 – pgs. 29, 32
Pray continually.

10) Romans 3:23 – pgs. 30, 54
For all have sinned and fall short of the glory of God.

11) Genesis 4:7 – pg. 31
If you do what is right, will you not be accepted? But if you do not do what is right, sin is crouching at your door; it desires to have you, but you must rule over it.

12) 1 Corinthians 6:19–20 – pg. 31
Do you not know that your bodies are temples of the Holy Spirit, who is in you, whom you have received from God? You are not your own;[20] you were bought at a price. Therefore honor God with your bodies.

13) Hebrews 13:4 – pg. 31
Marriage should be honored by all, and the marriage bed kept pure, for God will judge the adulterer and all the sexually immoral.

14) 1 John 1:9 – pg. 32
If we confess our sins, he is faithful and just and will forgive us our sins and purify us from all unrighteousness.

15) Psalm 25:14 – 20 – pg. 33
The Lord confides in those who fear him; he makes his covenant known to them. [15] My eyes are ever on the Lord, for only he will release my feet from the snare. [16] Turn to me and be gracious to me, for I am lonely and afflicted. [17] Relieve the troubles of my heart and free me from my anguish. [18] Look on my affliction and my distress and take away all my sins. [19] See how numerous are my enemies and how fiercely they hate me! [20] Guard my life and rescue me; do not let me be put to shame, for I take refuge in you.

16) John 10:10 – pg. 34
The thief comes only to steal and kill and destroy; I have come that they may have life, and have it to the full.

17) 1 John 4:4 – pg. 34
You, dear children, are from God and have overcome them, because the one who is in you is greater than the one who is in the world.

18) 1 Samuel 16:7 – pgs. 34 – 35
But the LORD said to Samuel, "Do not consider his appearance or his height, for I have rejected him. The LORD does not look at the things people look at. People look at the outward appearance, but the LORD looks at the heart."

19) Isaiah 54:5 – pg. 35
For your Maker is your husband—the LORD Almighty is his name—the Holy One of Israel is your Redeemer; he is called the God of all the earth.

20) Ecclesiastes 3:1 – pg. 37
There is a time for everything, and a season for every activity under the heavens:

21) Esther 4:14 – pg. 38
For if you remain silent at this time, relief and deliverance for the Jews will arise from another place, but you and your father's family will perish. And who knows but that you have come to your royal position for such a time as this?

22) Hebrews 11:1 – pgs. 43, 49
Now faith is confidence in what we hope for and assurance about what we do not see.

23) Hebrews 11:6 – pgs. 43, 49
And without faith it is impossible to please God, because anyone who comes to him must believe that he exists and that he rewards those who earnestly seek him.

24) Psalm 22:3 – pg. 47
Yet you are enthroned as the Holy One; you are the one Israel praises.

25) James 4:8 – pg. 48
Come near to God and he will come near to you. Wash your hands, you sinners, and purify your hearts, you double-minded.

26) Ephesians 3:20 – 21 – pg. 49
Now to him who is able to do immeasurably more than all we ask or imagine, according to his power that is at work within us, ^{21} to him be glory in the church and in Christ Jesus throughout all generations, for ever and ever! Amen.

27) John 17:15 – 16 – pg. 55
^{15} My prayer is not that you take them out of the world but that you protect them from the evil one. ^{16} They are not of the world, even as I am not of it.

28) Proverbs 14:12 – pg. 56
There is a way that appears to be right, but in the end it leads to death.

29) I Peter 3:3 – 4 – pgs. 57– 58
Your beauty should not come from outward adornment, such as elaborate hairstyles and the wearing of gold jewelry or fine clothes. ^{4} Rather, it should be that of your inner self, the unfading beauty of a gentle and quiet spirit, which is of great worth in God's sight.

30) I Peter 5:7 – pg. 58
Cast all your anxiety on him because he cares for you.

31) Psalm 24:1 – pg. 63
The earth is the Lord's, and everything in it, the world, and all who live in it;

32) I Peter 4: 8 – pg. 63
Above all, love each other deeply, because love covers over a multitude of sins.

33) Psalm 121:2 – pg. 66
My help comes from the Lord, the Maker of heaven and earth.

34) Luke 22:42 – pg. 74
"Father, if you are willing, take this cup from me; yet not my will, but yours be done."

35) Psalm 139:23 – pg. 74
Search me, God, and know my heart; test me and know my anxious thoughts.

36) Proverbs 18:22 – pg. 79
He who finds a wife finds what is good and receives favor from the Lord.

37) Matthew 19:25 – pg. 79
When the disciples heard this, they were greatly astonished and asked, "Who then can be saved?"

38) Proverbs 13:12 – pg. 82
Hope deferred makes the heart sick, but a longing fulfilled is a tree of life.

Lessons Learned

These are lessons that I have learned throughout during my Season of Preparation (SOP).

~~~~~~~~~~~~~~~~~~~~~~~~~~

Lesson Learned #1 : Let the Lord drive! Please! He is qualified to drive! pg. 19

Lesson Learned #2 : Don't settle for less than God's best for you… pg. 20

Learn Learned #3 : In the trenches: Everyone cannot stand in the trenches with you. pg. 21

Lesson Learned #4 : Check under your "personal hood" and see what is actually there. pg. 25

Lesson Learned #5 : As new believers in Christ, we must learn how to undo a lot of what we've done and believed for many years prior to becoming a Christian. pg. 27

Lesson Learned #6 : What a privilege to carry everything to God in prayer! pg. 28

Lesson Learned #7 : God knows all things, but He gives us choices…we have free will. pg. 31

Lesson Learned #8 : When we confess sin, we come into agreement with God on what He says about sin in our lives. pg. 32

Lesson Learned #9 : Continue to pray during your Season of Preparation! pg. 33

Lesson Learned #10 : …we all have room to practice patience in the area of waiting on God's timing. pg. 39

Lesson Learned #11 : Do not rush through things in your life, even during your Season of Preparation, that is leading you to your marriage. pg. 40

Lesson Learned #12 : A marriage God's way is multifaceted and can have a much bigger impact than we could ever know. pg. 41

Lesson Learned #13 : I'd rather be married to the right man at the right time and be the right woman when I get there. pg. 43

Lesson Learned #14 : Remember: Faith is required to please our Heavenly Father. pg. 43

Lesson Learned #15 : What this essentially means is that God wants me (and you) to wait on Him before entering into a relationship. pg. 44

Lesson Learned #16 : Always remember, you are okay, even if you do not have a significant other or a spouse right now! pg. 48

Lesson Learned #17 : When something comes up, deal with it! Deal with you! pg. 51

Lesson Learned #18 : Do not compromise yourself: No means, no! pg. 56

Lesson Learned #19 : God cares about you, Period! Always remember that! pg. 58

Lesson Learned #20 : A fact that we have all experienced in our lives at some point in time is that hurt people hurt other people. pg. 59

Lesson Learned #21 : God is able to "break negative behavior cycles" in our lives if we allow Him to do so. pg. 65

Lesson Learned #22 : Unhealthy connections are not worth wasting your time, energy, and life on! pg. 68

Lesson Learned #23 : As people, a lot of times, we try to fill voids in our lives with people, but only God can truly fill these voids! pg. 70

Lessons Learned #24 : He is so faithful! This point validates why we should always praise Him! pg. 73

Lesson Learned #25 : Making the decision on who you will marry is one of the most important life decisions that you will ever make. pg. 79

Lesson Learned #26 : God is our true provider and our source—He makes us complete. pg. 82

Thanks from author, Jacole Todd

The Season Continues

Thank you for taking this journey through Season of Preparation with me.

My heart's desire is that Season of Preparation has helped you in some way. As I have journeyed through my own personal (SOP), I am encouraged along the way as I take things one day at a time.

There are several resources and opportunities offered through Season of Preparation beyond the book.

Life coach sessions, social media and videos are some of the opportunities that are offered. See the social media listings below:

- Facebook: @SeasonofPreparation
- Twitter: @SeasonofPrep1
- Instagram: @seasonofpreparation
- YouTube: SeasonofPreparation

You may also email seasonofpreparation@gmail.com with any questions or inquiries for additional information.

Blessings to you on your Season of Preparation journey!

Jacole